SCHOLASTIC Phonics

Games

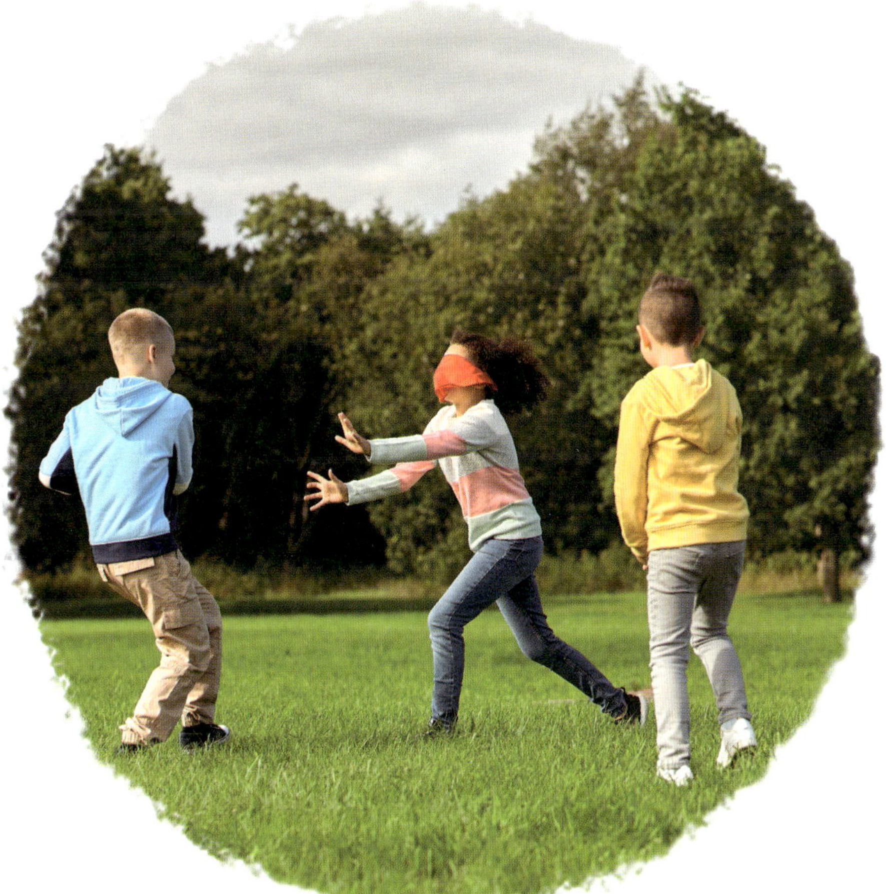

Published in the UK by Scholastic Education, 2023
Scholastic Distribution Centre, Bosworth Avenue, Tournament Fields, Warwick, CV34 6UQ
Scholastic Ireland, 89E Lagan Road, Dublin Industrial Estate, Glasnevin, Dublin, D11 HP5F

SCHOLASTIC and associated logos are trademarks and/or registered trademarks of Scholastic Inc.
www.scholastic.co.uk
© 2023 Scholastic
123456789 3456789012

Printed by Ashford Colour Press
The book is made of materials from well-managed, FSC®-certified forests and other controlled sources.

A CIP catalogue record for this book is available from the British Library.
ISBN 978-0702-32107-8

All rights reserved. This book is sold subject to the condition that it shall not, by way of trade or otherwise, be lent, hired out or otherwise circulated in any form of binding or cover other than that in which it is published. No part of this publication may be reproduced, stored in a retrieval system, or transmitted in any form or by any other means (electronic, mechanical, photocopying, recording or otherwise) without prior written permission of Scholastic.

Every effort has been made to trace copyright holders for the works reproduced in this publication, and the publishers apologise for any inadvertent omissions.

Author
Suzy Ditchburn

Editorial team
Rachel Morgan, Vicki Yates, Caroline Hale, Jennie Clifford

Design team
Dipa Mistry, Andrea Lewis, We Are Grace

Illustrations
Isabel Muñoz/The Bright Agency

Photographs
Cover Sezeryadigar/iStock
p4–5 twinsterphoto/iStock
p3, 6–7 Comeback Images/iStock
p1, 8–9 Ground Picture/Shutterstock
p8 (lightbulb) VectorCookies/iStock
p10–11, 24 Diego Cervo/Shutterstock
p16 XavierH/Shutterstock
p17 BasPhoto/Shutterstock
p18–19 South_agency/iStock
p20, 24 kali9/iStock
p21 CatbirdHill/Shutterstock

Help your child to read!

This book practises these letters and letter sounds.
Point and say the sounds with your child:

- o (as in 'most')
- i (as in 'minds')
- a (as in 'basic')
- a–e (as in 'games')
- i–e (as in 'time')
- o–e (as in 'rope')
- ew (as in 'new')

Your child may need help to read these common tricky words:

- are
- our
- the
- one
- their
- when
- someone
- you
- have
- to
- people
- by
- they
- all
- of
- your
- says

Before reading
- Look at the cover picture and read the title together. Read the back cover blurb to your child.
- Ask your child: *What games do you like playing?*
- Talk about the image in the magnifying glass.

During reading
- If your child gets stuck on a word, remind them to sound it out and then blend the sounds to read the word: o-v-er, over.
- If they are still stuck, show them how to read the word.
- Enjoy looking at the pictures together. Pause to talk about the information.

After reading
- Talk about the images on page 24. What can your child tell you about them?
- Ask your child: *How do you play hide-and-seek?*
- Discuss with your child their favourite game in the book and ask them to explain why.
- Discuss some of the games your child is less familiar with. Pilolo is a game from West Africa and one high kick is a game from Canada.

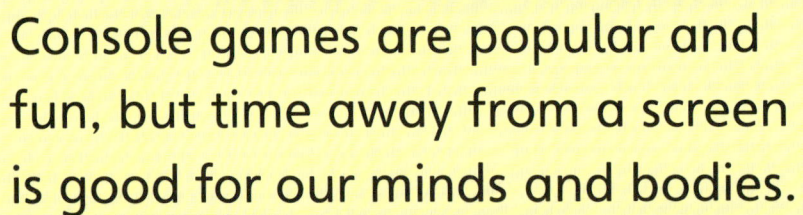

Console games are popular and fun, but time away from a screen is good for our minds and bodies.

Chasing Games

Tag is the most basic chasing game. One child is 'it' and chases their mates.

When that child tags someone, the new child is now 'it'.

You can play tag blindfolded, too (blind man's buff). You have to find people by hearing the sounds they make.

💡 In Mexico, this game is named the blind hen.

Hiding Games

Hide-and-seek is a popular game. A few people hide when someone counts alone.

Then the counter has to find them all.

In the game pilolo, stones or sticks are hidden for people to find.

It can be played with a few or lots of people.

Target Games
One foot high kick is an Inuit game.

A target is hung by a thin rope and players have to kick the target with one foot.

Thinking Games

If you prefer games that use your brain, how about chess?

Chess dates back about 1500 years.

Chess is good for the mind. You need to be smart to outplay your partner.

The game is over when the king is trapped and the winner says 'checkmate'.

Star checkers uses your brain, too.

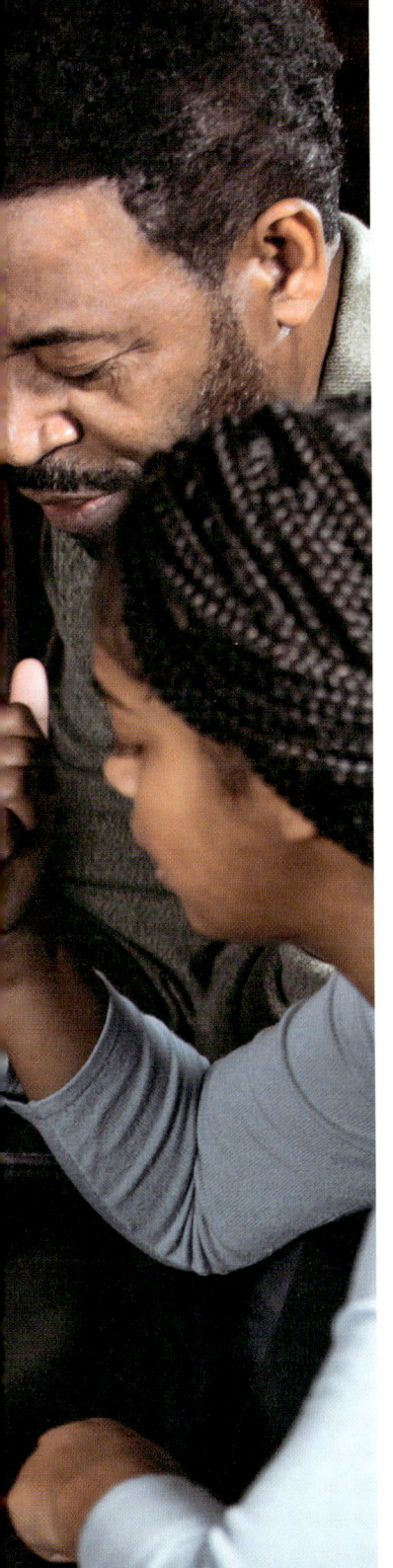

The aim is to be the first to get your ten pegs across to the opposing side.

If you like chasing, hiding or thinking, you might have found a few new games to play.

Talk about it!